Volume 05
Visualizing Architecture

V.05

Alex Hogrefe

www.visualizingarchitecture.com

ISBN 978-0-9913829-5-8

Contributors

Matt Uminski

Matt is a graphic designer based in Boston, Massachusetts. He has extensive experience in branding, print, and environmental design projects. Matt has worked with a range of public, institutional, higher education, and real estate clients on developing compelling brands that translate into real-world applications.

Jeff Kruth

Jeff is an urbanist and professor of architecture in Oxford, Ohio. His work focuses on the interface between architecture, the city, and the contributing forces that impact local economies and formulations of power and expertise.

Kimberly Hogrefe

My wife who has worked with me on this book through every step of the process. Without her, this book would not be possible.

14-41

Project 01: Research Lab

Located in the Alaskan wilderness, this design explores building in a dense forest landscape while minimizing environmental impact. The program is lifted into the tree canopy on pilotis and incorporates folding panel walls and green roofs.

42-73

Project 02: Philly Bridge

The bridge design connects an up-and-coming infrastructure project known as the Rail Park to the large convention center in the heart of Philadelphia. The bridge crosses over a busy highway incorporating parks, gardens, and retail into an active and engaging public experience.

74-103

Project 03: Desert Villa

The Desert Villa takes aggressive geometric forms and places them in the middle of the Nevada Salt Flats. The entire structure is recessed underground blurring the lines between building and landscape.

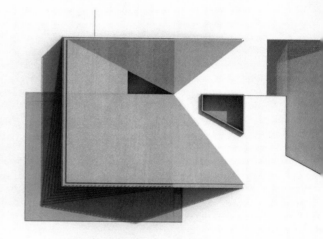

104-129

Project 04: Mountain Lodge

This 18-story tower is situated in the Swiss Alps near Trun, Switzerland. The lodge inserts guest suites and amenities into a slim and minimalist structure. A large oculus frames the view of both the nearby mountain and expansive Swiss landscape beyond.

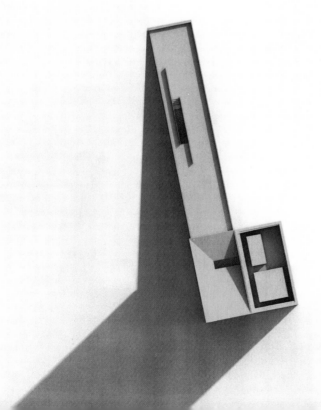

Preface

Portfolio Volume 05 represents nearly three years of experimentation and exploration into what it means to visualize architecture. Each portfolio I develop reflects current questions I am exploring in my own process and broader architectural visualization practices. In this particular volume I focused on questions of narrative and color. The process is always evolving, and each year, it is never the same. As my experience and understanding of visualization develops, my goals of what I am trying to achieve with my images inevitably shift.

For Portfolio Volume 05, I re-evaluated my priorities when it came to image-making. Architectural illustrations require knowledge across a broad spectrum of subjects. Design, technical implementation, color theory, lighting, composition, style, and storytelling are all elements constantly requiring resolution in every image. I work with many clients on many types of designs as well as find creative outlet through building images on my website and seeing how people respond to those images on social media. Through this type of engagement, my understanding of what makes a great architectural illustration has changed significantly. While I am continuing to practice and improve in all aspects of visualization, I spend less time developing my technical abilities and more time on the narrative of the images. It is through a focus on narrative elements that my images move closer to the kind of work I want to be producing. I try to emphasize these elements through this current volume.

In the past, I always approached visualization with the goal of making images feel more human. I emphasized the experiential and material qualities of architecture, as opposed to "out-of-the box" software rendering styles.

I would spend large amounts of my time refining my processes to move away from the seemingly "perfect" 3D representation to images that had sketchy and painterly qualities. I would use textures to manipulate the graphics, giving the appearance of smudges and imperfections. However, this approach was not clear in its intentions. My more recent focus on storytelling clarifies some of these ideas and allows more variety in the styles and approaches to architectural illustration. Ultimately, I find this approach better connects with audiences.

For this portfolio, an emphasis on storytelling meant focusing certain kinds of information and favoring bold images with a vivid palette on more minimal spreads. Images are spaced out and larger, filling the pages. This slows down the portfolio and encourages more time looking at individual images and graphics. In terms of production, this demands a higher quality and resolution, with focused execution and craft. Sometimes this means practicing restraint; trying to say more with less. And, sometimes, this means complexity, searching for how details might reveal something more about the design through the illustrations.

When discussing styles in architectural visualization with designers and students, the topic of photorealism inevitably reveals itself. While photorealism can go a long way in transporting a viewer to a place, it does not by itself provoke emotion or connect someone to a place. Over time, my work shifted to a more photorealistic look though this was not necessarily my intention. Rather, it was an inevitable outcome of refining my techniques to reveal more by building up layers of texture, light, and allowing composition to better define the images.

VA

For this portfolio, an emphasis on storytelling meant focusing certain kinds of information and favoring bold images with a vivid palette on more minimal spreads.

A juxtaposition of styles adjacent to each other in a portfolio draws out the unique qualities that each brings to the table. This relationship of different styles is what interests me most and is something that gives individuality and energy to a portfolio.

Many graphic styles are used throughout this book, and this is largely because I am genuinely interested in many styles of architectural illustrations. Photorealism, abstraction, diagrams, post-digital, and hand-drawn techniques can all be extremely compelling forms of visualization when executed properly to serve the intentions of the design. However, in my view, a portfolio consisting entirely of a single style tends to lack depth and eschews the inherent complexities associated with building in today's world. A juxtaposition of styles adjacent to each other in a portfolio draws out the unique qualities that each brings to the table. This relationship of different styles is what interests me most and is something that gives individuality and energy to a portfolio. The challenge of experimenting and developing narratives from such different forms of visualization perpetually excites me.

This portfolio contains four projects, each located in a unique environment. The different environments provide a set of parameters from which I can explore design and architectural graphics at multiple scales. As a professional architectural illustrator, I am always looking to expand my abilities and become a better artist, and these environments provide the framework from which I can test ideas and research different techniques. Each place also provides a context for not only the site design but also the overall mood and affect from which styles and graphics develop. The interplay of context and the graphics ultimately inform the overall design process. Therefore, the visualization is part of a rigorous and critical design process instead of simply an end result.

The specificity and uniqueness of each illustration, diagram, and graphic evoke a personality aligned with the design intent of the project and site. My goal is to design a portfolio that goes beyond a single style and concept, and allow for each project, and each spread within each project, to read independently. At the same time subtle organizing features such as common body text fonts and page numbers are implemented to tie the book together as a complete piece. I try to avoid as much as possible the automation and reproduction of styles and compositions. Instead graphics center around the uniqueness of each project. While more difficult, this approach of experimentation ultimately leads to a better understanding of visualization and gets me closer to what I think visualization and presentation of architecture should be.

The use of color is a central theme in this portfolio. I have always found that working with color is difficult and is something that I spend a lot of time practicing. Perhaps it is because of the infinite combinations or the layers of complexity they add to image-making. I have also come to realize its importance to the success of visualization. This portfolio marks my attempt to better understand and work with color through toning, combinations, and the strength of subtlety through color. Feeling comfortable with color is still part of a growing process, but during the creation of Portfolio Volume 05, I began to understand how subtle shifts in color and tone can significantly alter the narrative of the graphic.

Most advice on the creation of architecture portfolios is insufficient, often resulting in a "checklist" mentality, which does not suit most designers, or allow a portfolio to be a unique constructed work in itself. Most advice surrounding portfolios is didactic, saying "Do this, not this." In my view there cannot be a single blueprint to creating a portfolio. They are incredibly personal. And thus, they cannot simply be copies of other layouts or styles or the unfortunate end result of a checklist. Instead, I propose to offer a point of departure, a place to start. I find inspiration all over, in many places, and in many forms. I draw inspiration from photographers, graphic designers, and advertisers. I find inspiration in books, on tv, and social media. And when I find inspiration, the ideas start running. Where I start is almost never where I finish.

The illustrations and spreads in this book are the result of multiple iterations. When I start with an idea, I will sometimes create five, ten, or even fifteen versions to study several possibilities. These are versions looking at color, style, composition, story, texture, et cetera. I then take the best idea, push it forward, and then iterate again. Sometimes, I will have several versions moving alongside each other simultaneously. Sometimes, I abandon an idea that I have worked on for weeks, and completely start over. Eventually, I need to choose a path and stick to it.

This is often the unfortunate but necessary process of worthy design. This effort of testing and iterating always pays dividends at the end and leads to a more personal representation of work.

I primarily used three software programs to generate the illustrations in this book. SketchUp was utilized to model all 3-D content including the architecture, context, and occasionally for vegetation,vehicles, and base content for diagrams. I used V-Ray for all of my 3-D model rendering. While it is primarily used to generate high-quality base images for my perspective illustrations, I also render clay model images as bases for diagramming. Finally, Photoshop is used for post-production of the base rendering, ultimately giving life and depth to the illustrations. On average, 50-75% of my time is spent in Photoshop. Photoshop is where I refine textures, insert most of the vegetation and entourage, and layer in the atmospheric and lighting effects. However, these specific software programs described above are by no means required to create the same quality of images seen in this portfolio. The process and fundamentals matter most, and these ideas are transferable to almost any software.

Most advice surrounding portfolios is didactic, saying "Do this, not this." In my view there cannot be a single blueprint to creating a portfolio. They are incredibly personal.

Research Lab

Fairbanks, Alaska

VA

Situated in the pristine Alaskan wilderness, the Research Lab sits in a valley just to the west of Fairbanks, Alaska. Here, birch trees wrap the site in a densely covered canopy. In close proximity to both the nearby international airport and amid shifting ecologies, the site provides opportunities for climatic and ecological research in Alaska.

Much of the Alaskan frontier is rapidly changing due to many factors, including the stresses of climate change. The intensity and speed of the changing environment require a space that allows for research to occur in the region and an architecture with a minimal impact on that environment. The Research Lab thus implements several sustainable and performative aspects to be self-sufficient.

The design takes direct cues from its surroundings. The wood material that makes up the skin of the building mimics the surrounding black and white bark patterns of the Betula papyrifera (Paper Birch) trees. This is not to camouflage but rather to acknowledge the forest. The architecture is rounded and smoothed at the base and then transitions to sharp orthogonal forms above— freeing the ground plane, while immersing researchers and visitors amid the canopy of the trees. The building reveals itself through layers of privacy, views and lighting. The glazing, for example, is fritted to prevent solar gain, as well as to avoid confusion for aviary wildlife, preventing birds from hitting the glass. At night, the screened glazing provides privacy while diffusing the light.

Instead of removing trees to make way for the structure, the structure is built around the existing trees. The design weaves, bobs, and tucks, allowing for a meaningful integration with the site. Thus, architecture becomes a platform from which to observe the landscape beyond as well as the landscape within itself.

Access to the lab occurs through two cores on opposing ends of the structure. Each core contains a stair and elevator. The lab itself is made up of two levels. Level 1 houses program such as living quarters, a shared kitchen, lab space, office space, and conference rooms. An open-air corridor follows the southern facade where large folding screens can be opened and closed to admit light and fresh air into the structure. Level 2 contains a large green roof and deck space. There is also a glass pavilion on the roof serving as a multipurpose space for the researchers.

Research requires many levels of privacy. This idea of opacity and transparency has been carried over into the entire facade of the structure. Every panel folds to create an entirely open or closed position, giving the user full control over light, sound, and air coming in and out of the spaces. The panels themselves are perforated to provide 90% light filtering. The complete control of the porosity of the facade gives researchers maximum flexibility of privacy and environmental connection while allowing for insulation and variations in light conditions.

Instead of removing trees to make way for the structure, the structure is built around the existing trees. The design weaves, bobs, and tucks, allowing for a meaningful integration with the site.

Birch Forest

⊕ **Site Location**

N

-10 miles

0

10 miles

20 miles

30 miles

VA

Fairbanks,
Alaska

Elevation: 446 ft.

Population: 31,500

Annual High Temp: 38° F / 3° C

Annual Low Temp: 17° F / -8° C

Average Rain: 11 in. per year

Average Snow: 65 in. per year

Fairbanks

Alaska

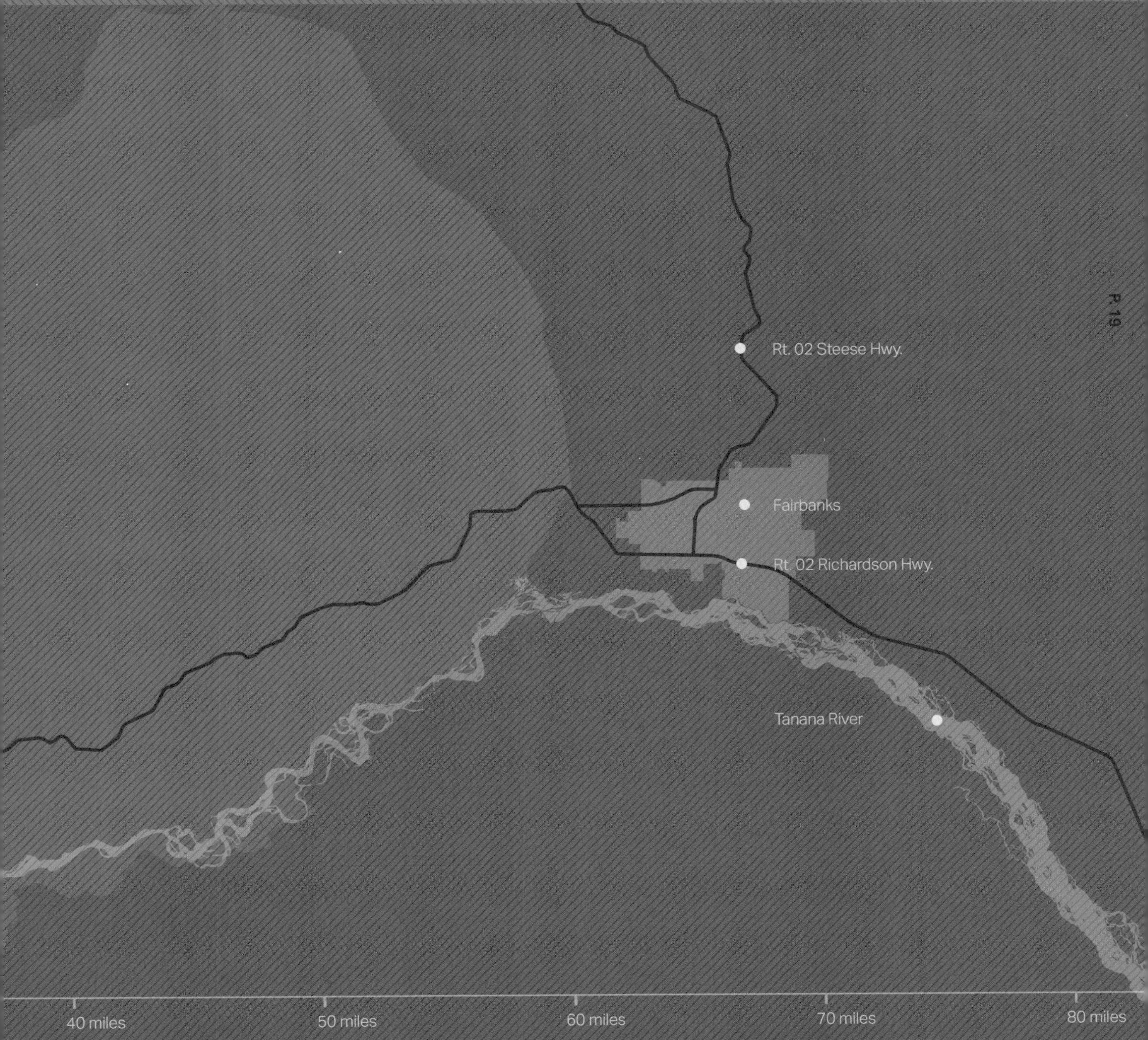

Rt. 02 Steese Hwy.

Fairbanks

Rt. 02 Richardson Hwy.

Tanana River

40 miles   50 miles   60 miles   70 miles   80 miles

Form 01   **Form 02**   **Form 03**   **Form 04**

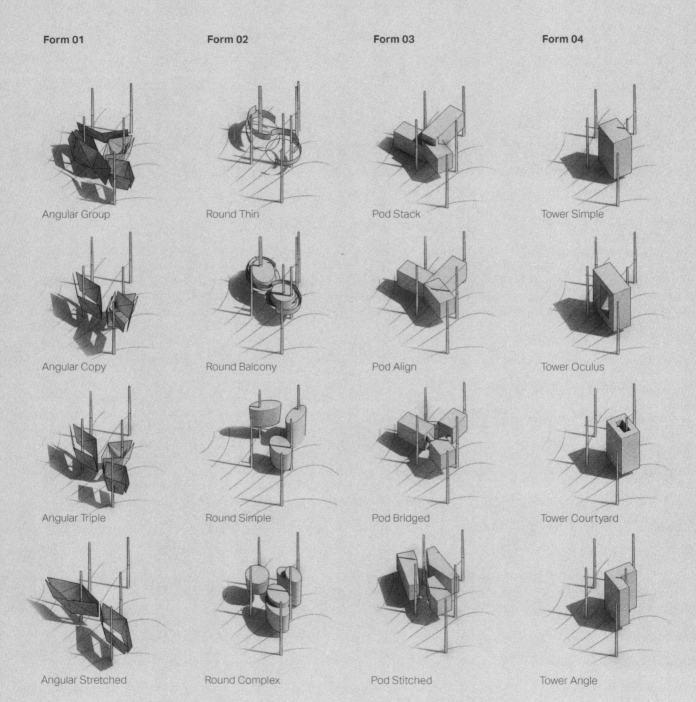

Angular Group   Round Thin   Pod Stack   Tower Simple

Angular Copy   Round Balcony   Pod Align   Tower Oculus

Angular Triple   Round Simple   Pod Bridged   Tower Courtyard

Angular Stretched Round Complex   Pod Stitched   Tower Angle

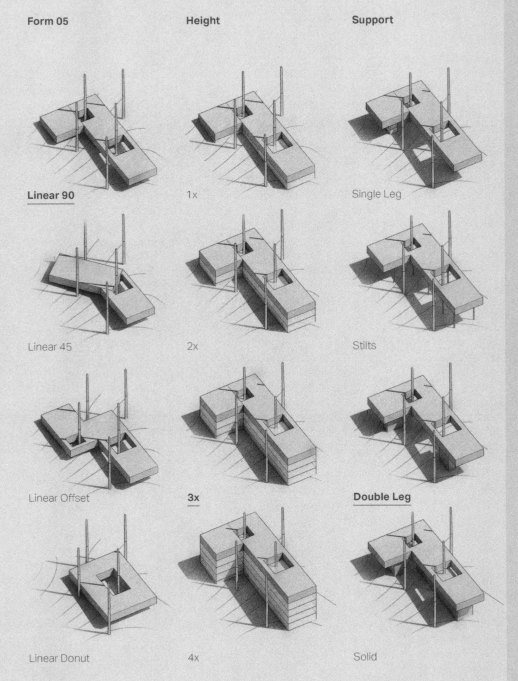

Form 05

Height

Support

Linear 90

1x

Single Leg

Linear 45

2x

Stilts

Linear Offset

3x

Double Leg

Linear Donut

4x

Solid

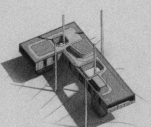

Final

Linear 90
3x
Double Leg

The structure is lifted by three columnar supports. Elevating the lab well off the ground minimizes its impact on the existing site conditions and lets the ecology flow below it.

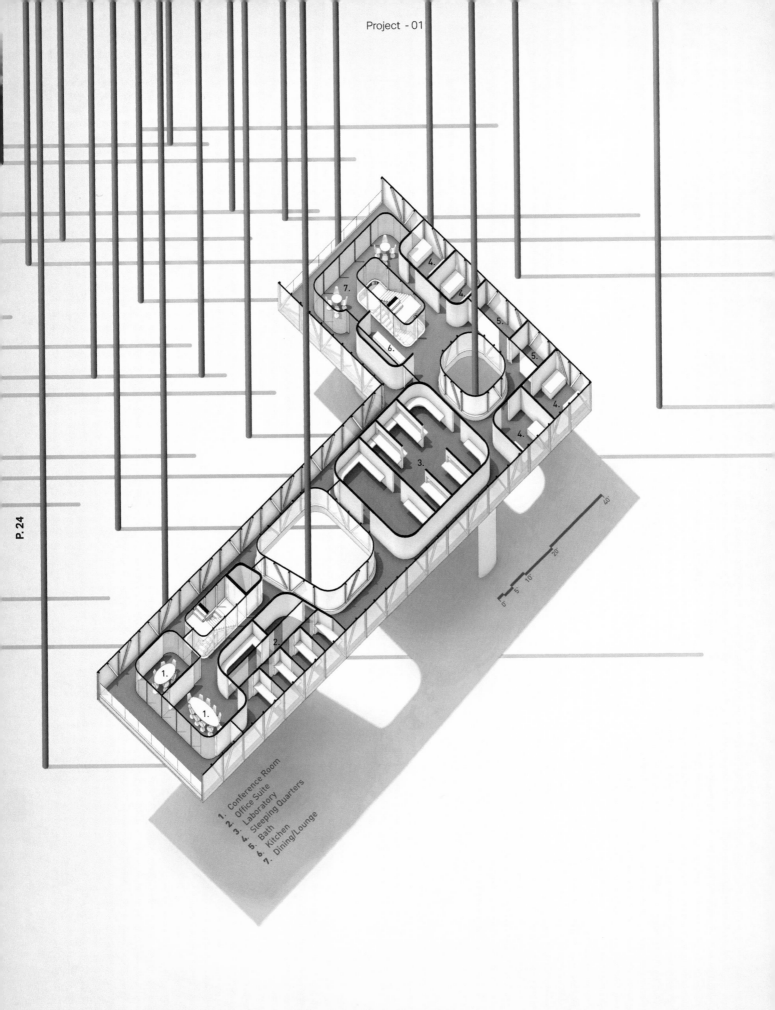

1. Conference Room
2. Office Suite
3. Laboratory
4. Sleeping Quarters
5. Bath
6. Kitchen
7. Dining/Lounge

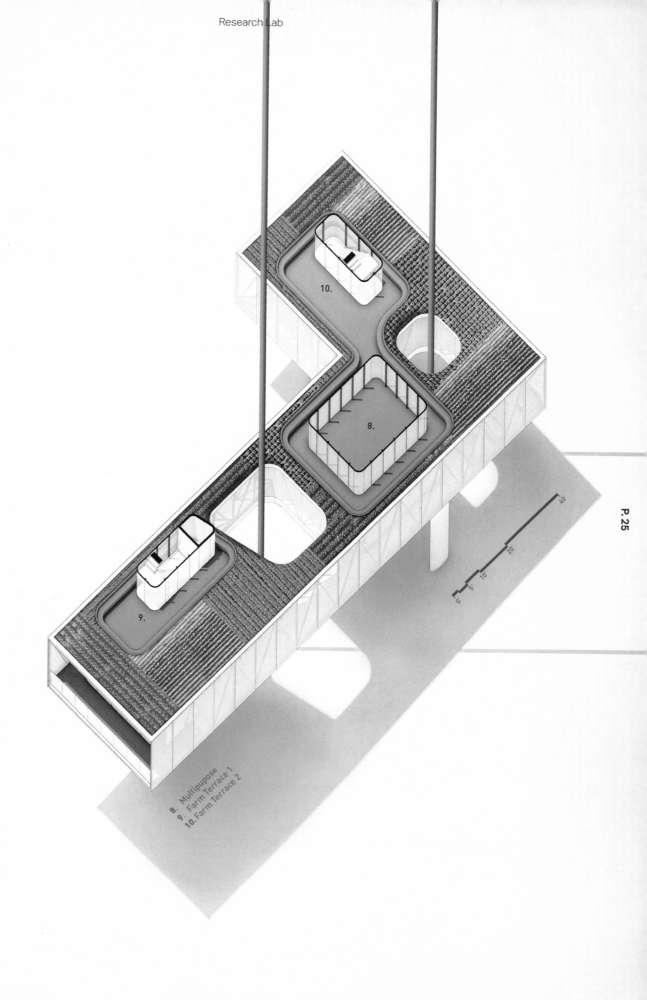

8. Multipupose
9. Farm Terrace 1
10. Farm Terrace 2

Returning From Research: View from South

Top Left
Conference Rooms

Top Right
Tree Cutout

Bottom Right
Open Air Corridor

Roof Gardens and Social Space: Bird's-eye View

1. Stair
2. Elevator
3. Conference Rooms
4. Labotories
5. Multipurpose Room
6. Garden
7. Crow's Nest

Light Infiltration

Floor to ceiling panels wrap every exterior facade maximizing light into the space. Lab space is located in the center of the building where privacy and light control is needed most. Social spaces such as living quarters and conference rooms are placed at each end of the structure, giving access to balconies and outdoor space.

Top Right
Leaving for an Excursion

Bottom
Translucent Panels Closeup

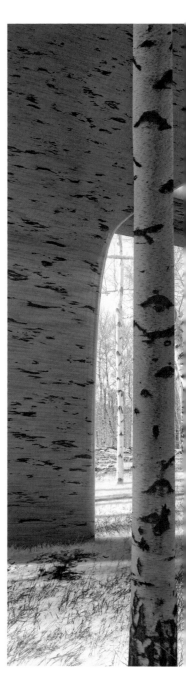

Fully Open Panels

Shaded Semi-Open Panels

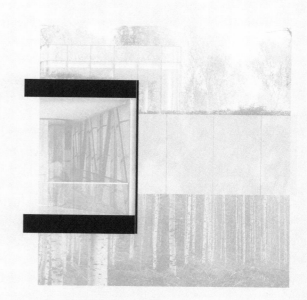

Pinhole Semi-Private Panels

Fully Closed Panels

P. 38

Fully Closed Panels: View from the South

P. 40

Fully Open Panels: View from the South

P.41

PHILLY BRIDGE

Philadelphia, Pennsylvania

From the highway, the fluid curves of the bridge suggest a new civic identity for Philadelphia's infrastructure. Glass platforms project outwards from the underside of the bridge, hinting at the exciting activities above and urging passersby to pull off the highway and explore the bridge.

Philadelphia is a beautiful city with a rich history. Much is being done in the city to rethink its public realm and park system. While the city maintains many of its historic landmarks, some have been ignored or deemed obsolete. However, a new movement has surfaced in the city to rehabilitate an old elevated rail line. Similar to New York's Highline, the Rail Park project has begun renovation of a three-mile stretch, offering pedestrians unobstructed views and new paths through the city. A quarter-mile mile stretch of the project (Phase 01) is already complete.

A major design challenge for the Philly Bridge is in connecting the Rail Park to the energetic core of the city. As it stands now, Interstate 676 acts as a barrier between the Rail Park and the convention center area. While ground level pedestrian bridges cross the interstate, they still privilege automobile transport. Large expanses of concrete and asphalt act as a deterrent to pedestrians.

The Philly Bridge spans across the roadway at the Rail Park level away from vehicular traffic. Large grand stairs will lower to new parks on both sides of the highway, providing buffers from the harsh urban edges. The identity of the bridge changes from day to night. During the day, the Bridge is inviting, relaxed, and vibrant.

Visitors promenade through the many pocket parks, kids play soccer, and runners choose their favorite routes. At night, the energy of the Bridge shifts when the lights come on, and the colors on the bridge play an important role in creating a more filmic identity within the city. The city lights become a backdrop to vibrant retail and outdoor cafes and a civic nightlife emerges.

People cross the bridge using one of three unique routes. The first route leads through a labyrinth of gardens filled with native plant species meant to educate and connect with the adjacent parks and landscapes. The second route wraps to the other side of the bridge crossing open grass fields creating a place of recreation and relaxation. Finally, the third route runs through the center of the bridge offering a retail corridor flanked with restaurants and boutique shops.

From the highway, the fluid curves of the bridge suggest a new civic identity for Philadelphia's infrastructure. Glass platforms project outwards from the underside of the bridge, hinting at the exciting activities above and urging passersby to pull off the highway and explore the bridge. At night, this beacon intensifies when its lighting features dance around the copper curved panels. To walk across these platforms is to experience the phenomena and dynamism of urban life.

01

0 mi.

10

25

50

100

New Haven

New York

Easton

Allentown

Reading

Princeton

Trenton

Brick

Philadelphia

Toms River

Cherry Hill

35 mi.

Atlantic

55 mi.

MAP **02**

Newark   Wilmington

80 mi.

Vineland

Atlantic City

Ocean City

Dover

Cape May

Easton

Lewes

N

Philadelphia,
Pennsylvania

Elevation: 39 ft.
Population: 1,584,000
Annual High Temp: 65° F / 18° C
Annual Low Temp: 47° F / 8°C
Average Rain: 42 in. per year
Average Snow: 23 in. per year

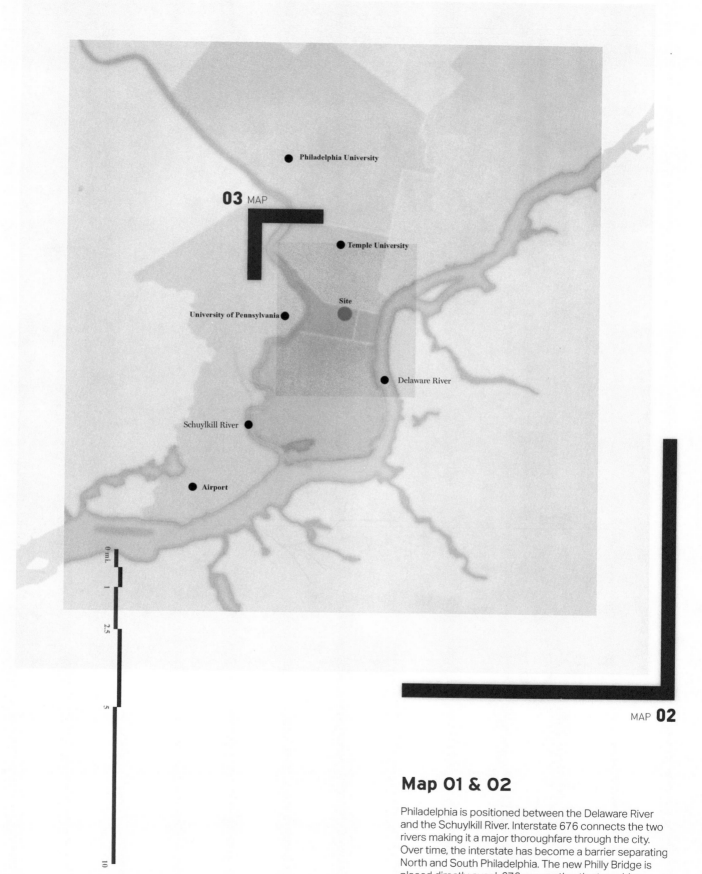

Philadelphia University

03 MAP

Temple University

Site

University of Pennsylvania

Delaware River

Schuylkill River

Airport

0 mi.
1
2.5
5
10

MAP **02**

Map 01 & 02

Philadelphia is positioned between the Delaware River and the Schuylkill River. Interstate 676 connects the two rivers making it a major thoroughfare through the city. Over time, the interstate has become a barrier separating North and South Philadelphia. The new Philly Bridge is placed directly over I-676 connecting the two sides.

03 MAP

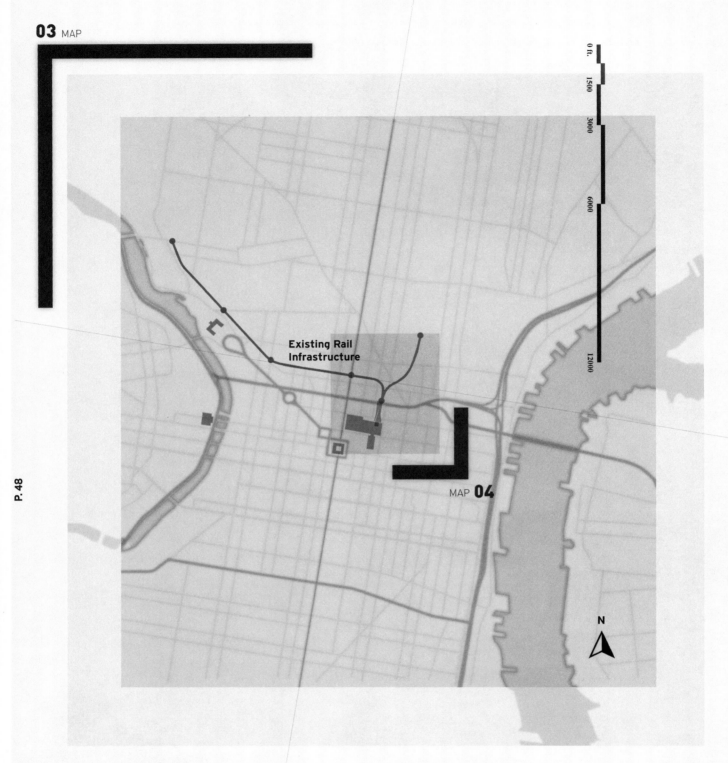

Existing Rail Infrastructure

MAP **04**

N

Map 03 & 04

The existing rail infrastructure is expansive but largely lives on the north side of I-676. However, a small part of the rail bends south near the Pennsylvania Convention Center. It is at this location that the new bridge connects to the existing rail and crosses over to the city center.

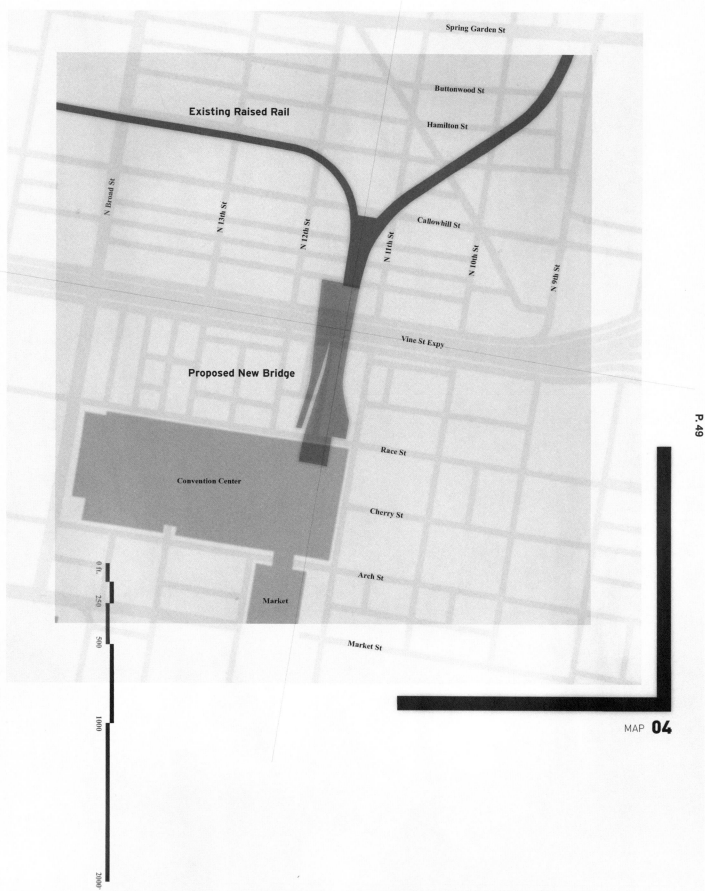

Spring Garden St

Buttonwood St

Hamilton St

Existing Raised Rail

N Broad St

N 13th St

N 12th St

Callowhill St

N 11th St

N 10th St

N 9th St

Vine St Expy

Proposed New Bridge

Race St

Convention Center

Cherry St

Arch St

Market

Market St

0 ft.

250

500

1000

2000

MAP **04**

City Hall

R.T. Market

Pennsylvania Convention Center

P. 50

Proposed Philly Bridge

I-676

Phase 01
Completed Section
of New Rail Park Project

Existing Viaduct

VA

Philly Bridge

I-76

I-676

Existing Underground Tunnel Rail

Existing Recessed Rail

Rail Park

The Philly Bridge cannot be discussed without first discussing the Rail Park Project. A revitalization of the rail infrastructure shown in orange is already underway. Phase 01 of the Rail Park is now complete, showcasing newly planted landscape, paths, and oversized industrial swings. The completed section is a quarter-mile mile long and has two access points from the street. The project is both publicly and privately funded and plans to stretch the entire three mile rail from the viaduct to the tunnel rail connecting ten neighborhoods and fifty city blocks.

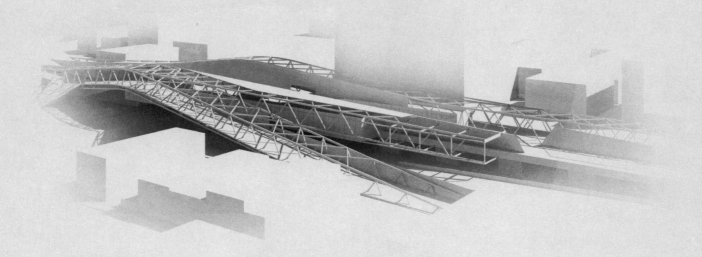

Industrial

Early on, the design took on an industrial look with lots of exposed steel trusses. The idea was that this styling would respond to the qualities of the historic rail lines. However, the exposed structure gave the bridge a complexity that overpowered the context, and this visual identity was overhauled for a simpler, contemporary look

Contemporary

This cleaner design emphasizes the curves of the bridge and gives the project a modern feel. The minimal design shifts focus from the structure to the programmatic elements, thus clarifying their implementation.

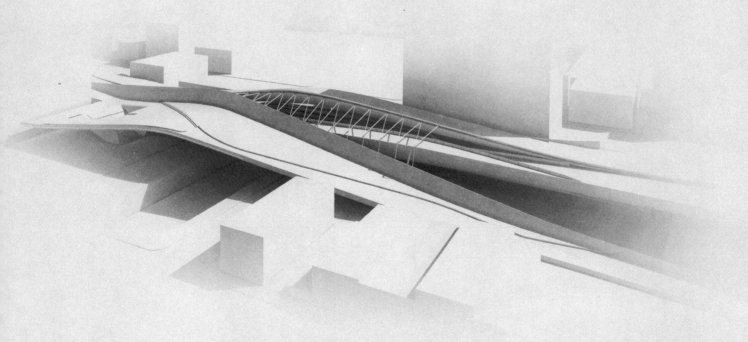

Existing Conditions

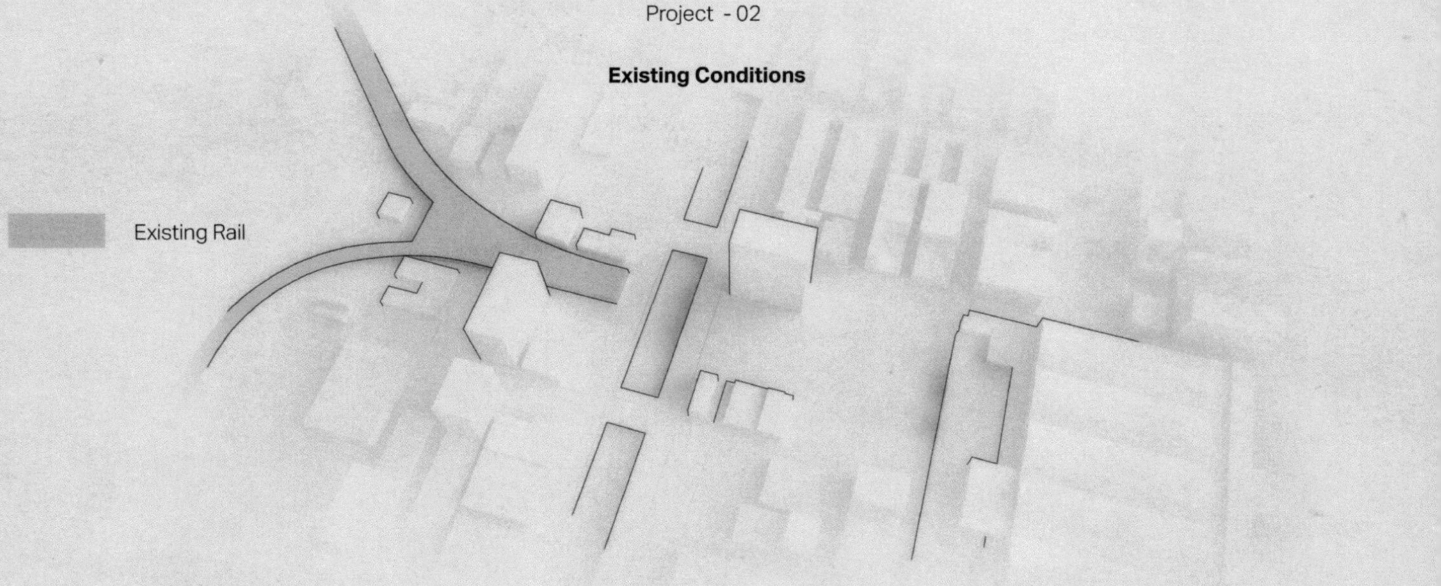

Existing Rail

Vehicular Traffic

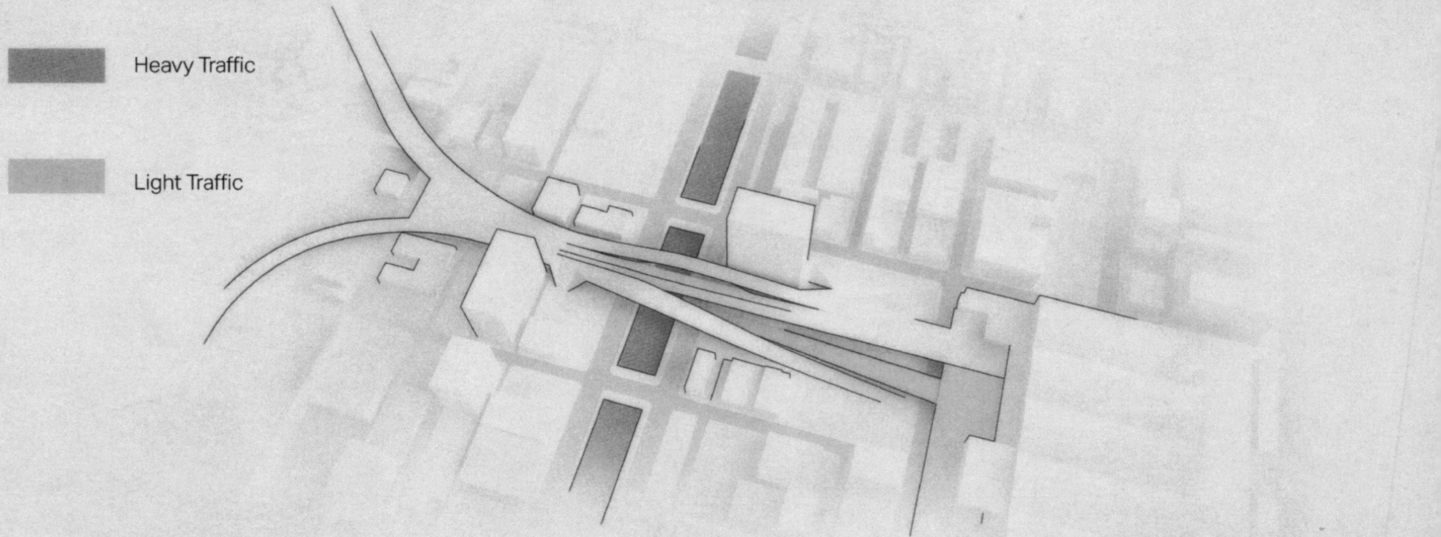

Heavy Traffic

Light Traffic

Garden Path

Pedestrian Paths

Retail Path

Park Path

VA

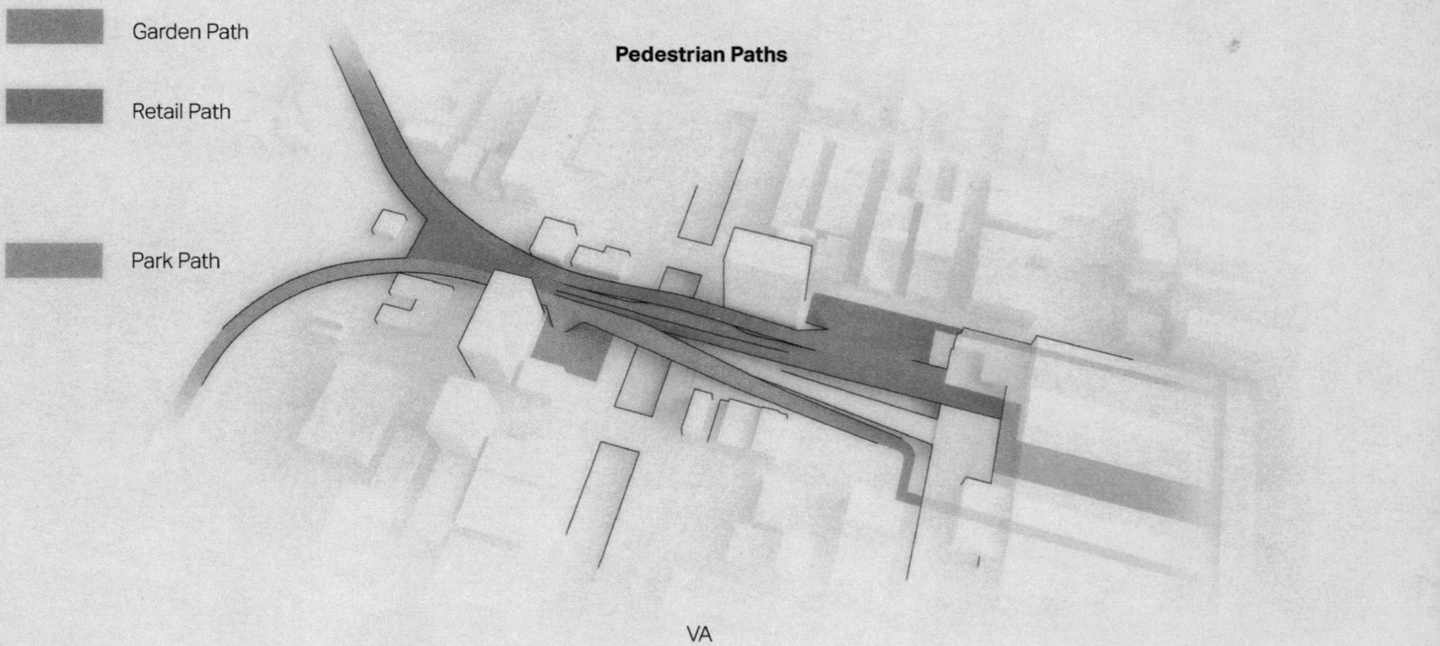

Green Space

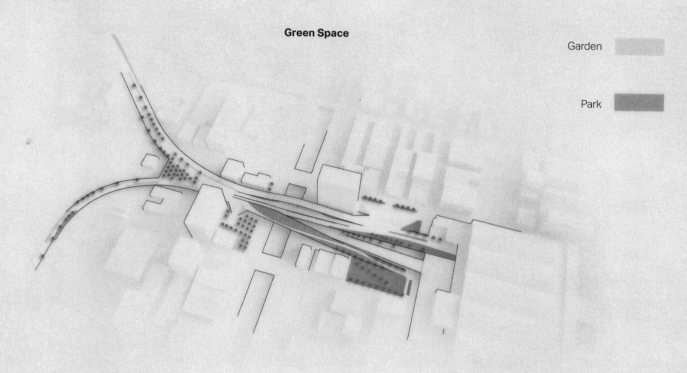

Garden

Park

Street Connection

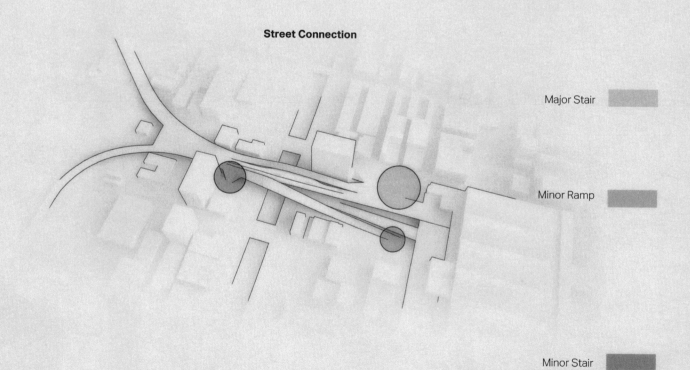

Major Stair

Minor Ramp

Minor Stair

Kite Festival: View from the West

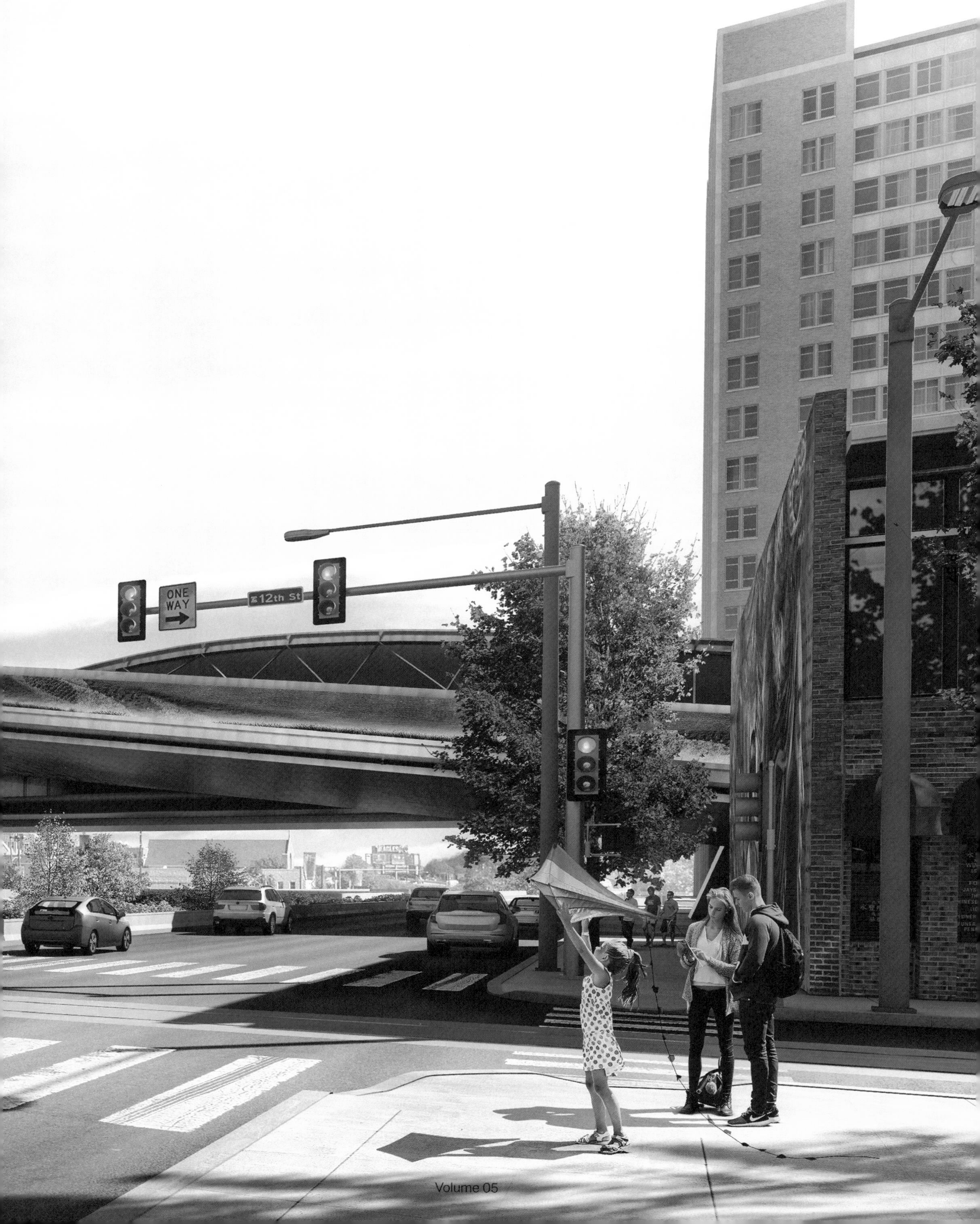
ONE
WAY
12th St

Section Perspective C-C

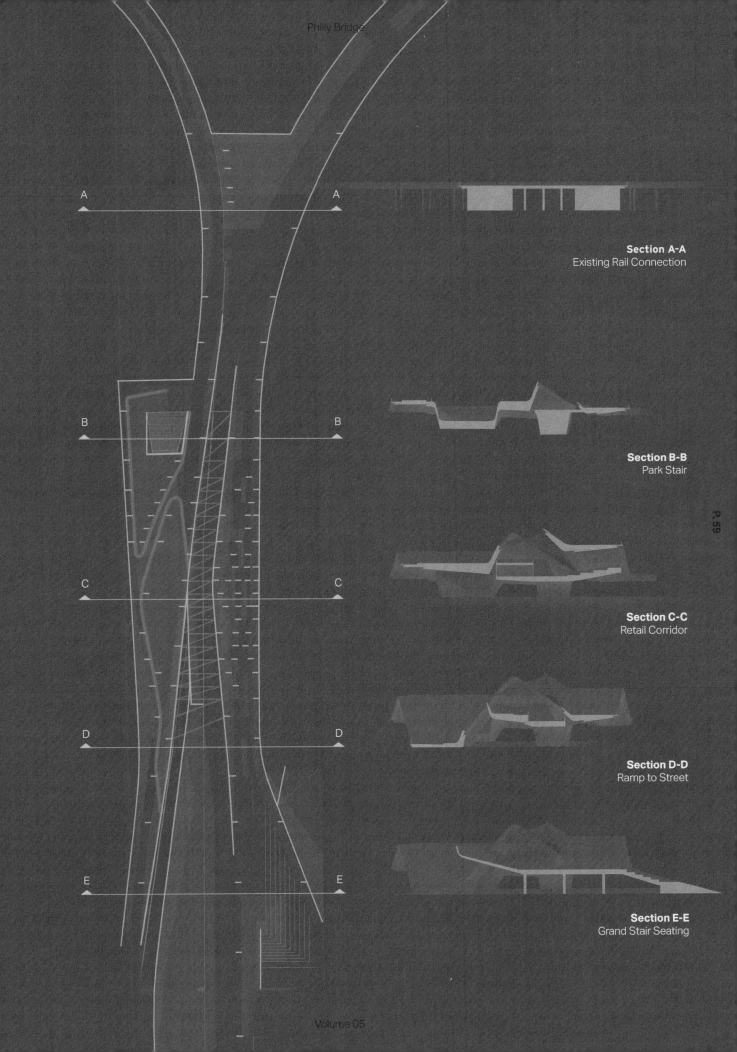

Philly Bridge

A ———————————— A

Section A-A
Existing Rail Connection

B ———————————— B

Section B-B
Park Stair

C ———————————— C

Section C-C
Retail Corridor

D ———————————— D

Section D-D
Ramp to Street

E ———————————— E

Section E-E
Grand Stair Seating

Highway Perspective: View from the West

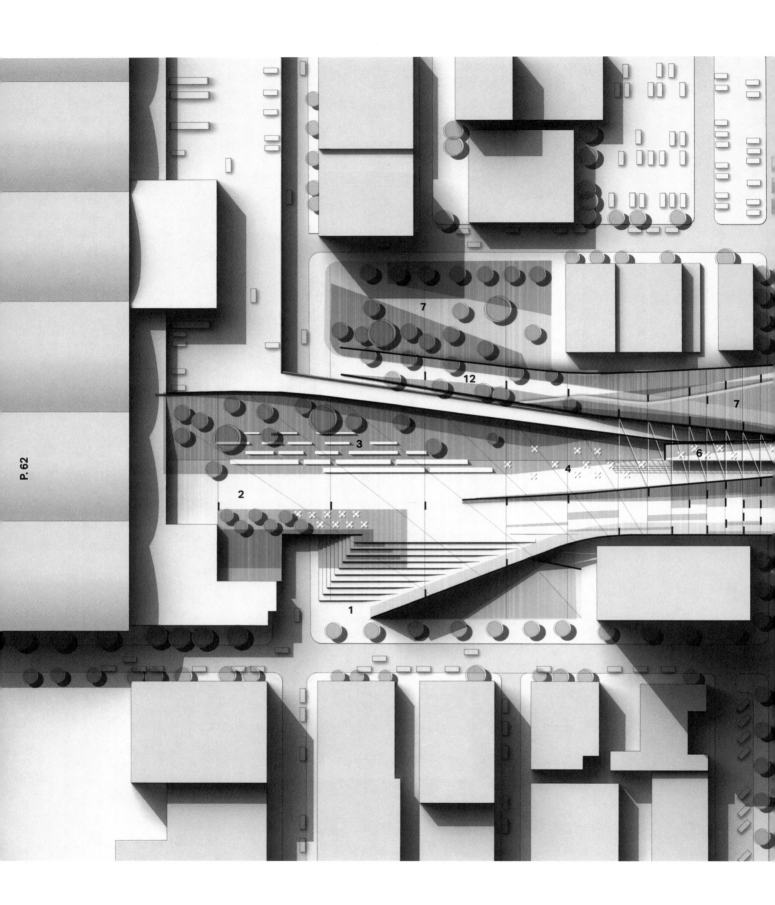

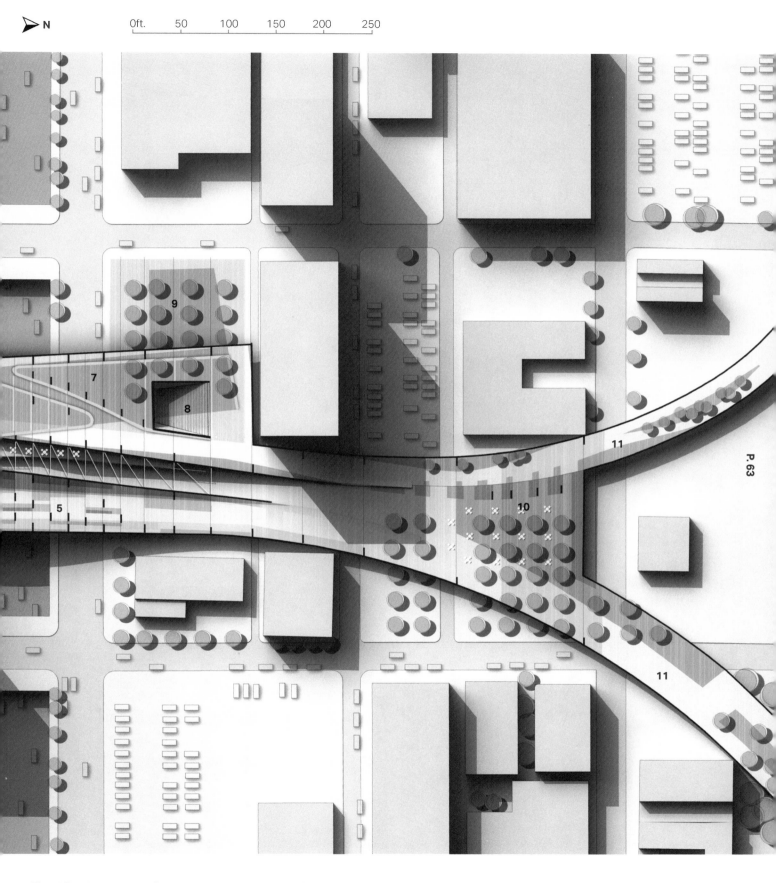

N

0ft.   50   100   150   200   250

P. 63

1. Tiered Seating   5. Gardens   9. Lower Bosque
2. Convention Entry   6. Retail   10. Upper Bosque
3. Wild Grass   7. Park   11. Existing Rail
4. Outdoor Cafe   8. Stairs   12. Ramp

Serene Evening: South Grand Stair

Seasonal Acitivities: West Upper Park

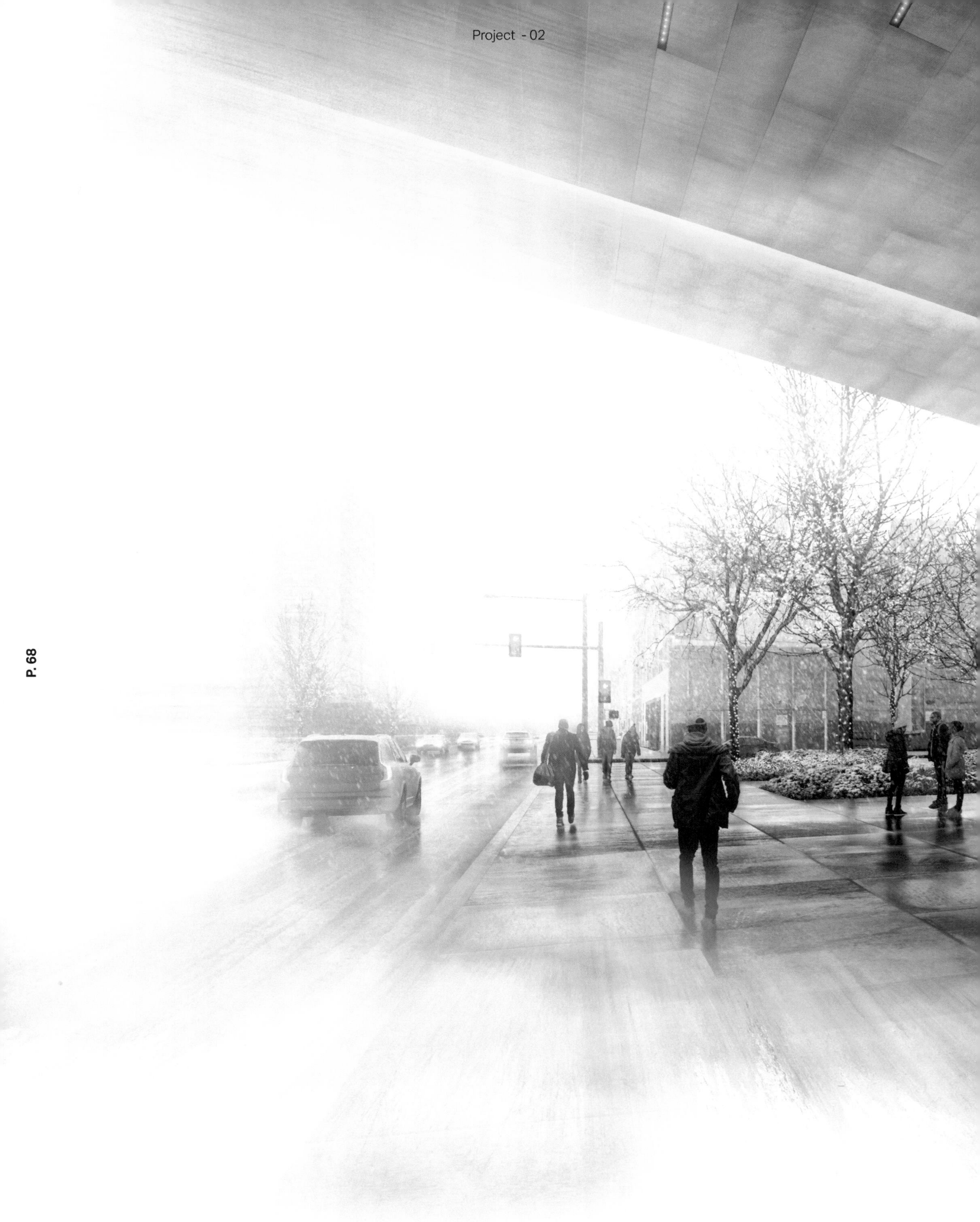

P. 69

Sled Excursion: North Stair

Finding Shade: Retail Corridor in the Afternoon

Street Performance: Retail Corridor at Night

Philly Bridge: Aerial View from the East

VA

Desert Villa

Black Rock Desert, Nevada

This house, located in the salt flats of Nevada, inserts a sharp and intense geometry into the minimal and expansive environment. It acts as a sunken oasis within the barren landscape. The contrast of the extremely flat ground with strong cantilevered forms willfully plays off the sharp mountain formations in the distant horizon. The program is recessed 12 feet below the salt flat surface, allowing the roofs to slope to the ground and integrate with the earthwork while recalling the nearby rock formations.

Approaching the building, one realizes the ground peels away to reveal stairs descending to the entrances. Though the architectural forms contrast with the site, the materials help to connect with the landscape. The sloped roofs maintain the same soil and salt composition of the site itself, blurring the line between architecture and landscape. Louvers and flooring are constructed of regional wood species. Textured plaster cover the interior walls. The simple set of natural materials are meant to evoke a sense of simplicity and warmth.

The form draws inspiration from the origami-like folding of paper. Similar to paper, the folds offer strength and triangulate the large flat surfaces allowing for large spans and overhangs. Conceptually, the design started with a simple cube form from which pieces were pinched, pulled, and folded. The resulting form changes significantly depending on the position of the observer.

Two large courtyards in the center of the floor plan form an interior oasis of vegetation and allow for natural ventilation. These courtyards also bring light deep into the interior spaces of the house, as well as provide a controlled environment for gardening. The roofs of the house all slope toward the center bringing much needed rain into the courtyards. The gardens also spill over into the recessed hardscapes around the exterior perimeter of the living space. All walls surrounding the courtyard and exterior hardscapes are glass, blurring the line between inside and out.

As one approaches the building, passive solar design elements begin to appear. Roofs cantilever more than 80 feet to shade large swaths of hardscape and landscape of the sunken plaza below. Louvers provide shading and diffuse natural light, reducing thermal heat gain. Inside, thick masonry walls are strategically placed acting as thermal masses to absorb heat during the day and release it at night.

The form draws from origami-like folds in paper. Similar to paper, the folds offer strength and triangulate the large flat surfaces allowing for large spans and overhangs.

**Site
Location**

0mi

5

10

15

20

VA

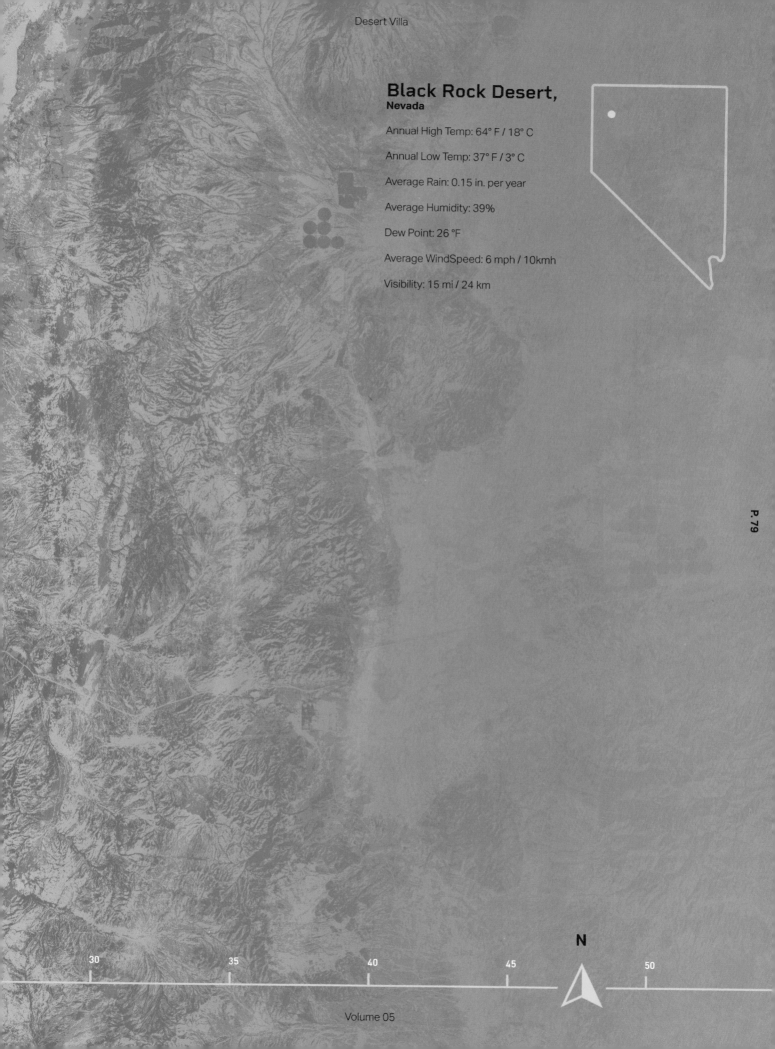

Black Rock Desert,
Nevada

Annual High Temp: 64° F / 18° C

Annual Low Temp: 37° F / 3° C

Average Rain: 0.15 in. per year

Average Humidity: 39%

Dew Point: 26 °F

Average WindSpeed: 6 mph / 10kmh

Visibility: 15 mi / 24 km

N

30   35   40   45   50

Infinite Runway: Plan View

Just Landed: View from the West

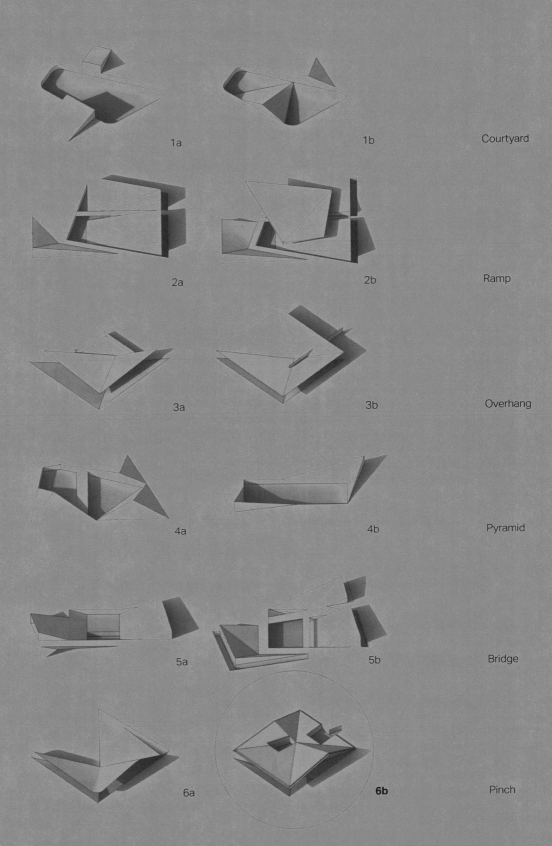

1a

1b

Courtyard

2a

2b

Ramp

3a

3b

Overhang

4a

4b

Pyramid

5a

5b

Bridge

6a

6b

Pinch

Desert Villa

Ground Pinch

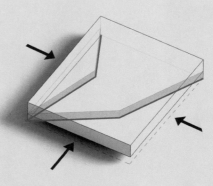

Overhang Pinch

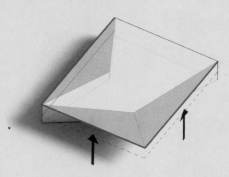

Back Pinch

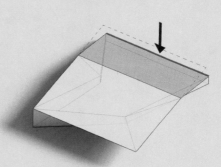

Center Roof Pinch

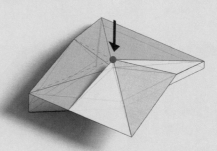

Building Recess

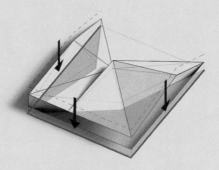

Form Rotation Illustrations

Pure Reflection

One of the naturally occurring events of the salt flats is its seasonal shallow flooding. The desert house perimeter hardscape is lifted slightly to shed water during the winter months when flooding is most prevalent. During heavy flood events, the house becomes an island surrounded by water. The landscape becomes an uninterrupted mirrored surface for miles in all directions. These silvery reflections offer an experience only a few places in the world provide.

VA

P. 90

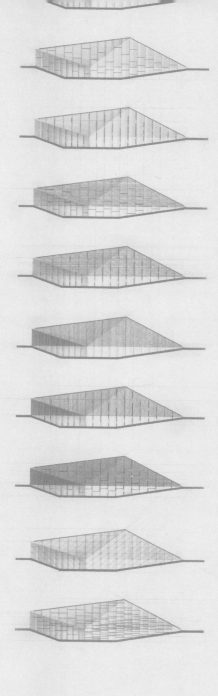

Wood Louver Pattern Studies

The wood louvers not only act as an important passive solar heat strategy but also as a textural and design element. Several patterns were studied to determine the best compromise between form and function. Ultimately, simplicity won out. The form of the villa is very angular and aggressive. Therefore, a simple louver pattern provides the best backdrop to emphasize the geometry instead of drawing attention away from it.

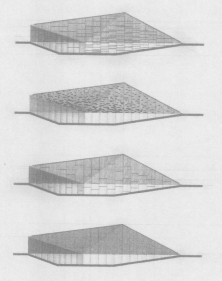

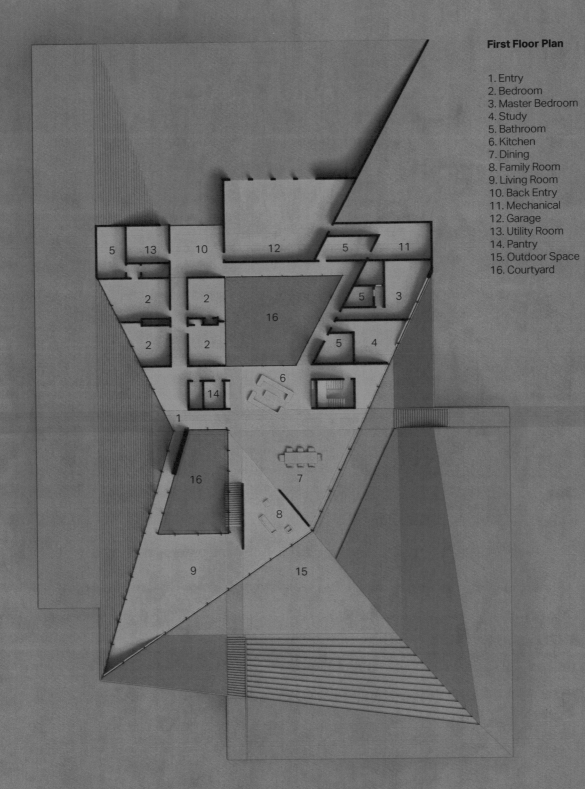

First Floor Plan

1. Entry
2. Bedroom
3. Master Bedroom
4. Study
5. Bathroom
6. Kitchen
7. Dining
8. Family Room
9. Living Room
10. Back Entry
11. Mechanical
12. Garage
13. Utility Room
14. Pantry
15. Outdoor Space
16. Courtyard

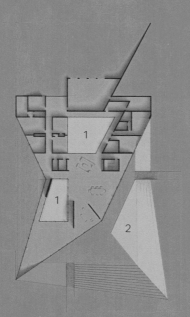

Green Space

1. Garden
2. Native Plantings

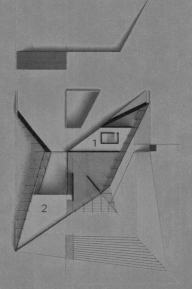

Second Floor Plan

1. Roof Access
2. Loft

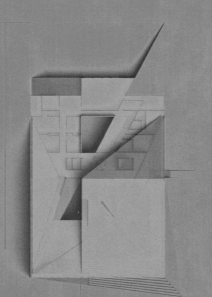

Roof Plan

Spacial Studies: Kitchen

Spacial Studies: Living Room

Light Studies: Kitchen

Light Studies: Living Room

Garden Paths: Sunken Entry View

Building Section: A-A

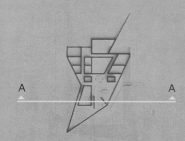

A ——————————————— A

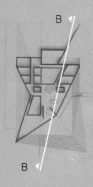

B

B

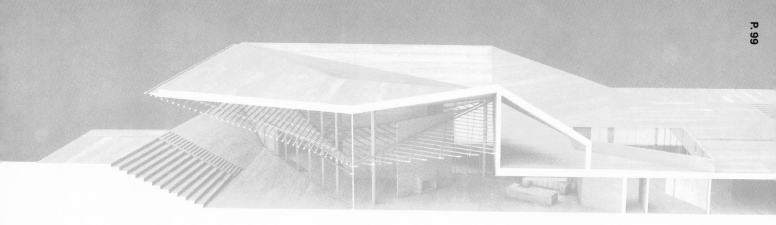

Building Section: B-B

Dust Storm: View from the Southwest

Cool Lantern: View from the East

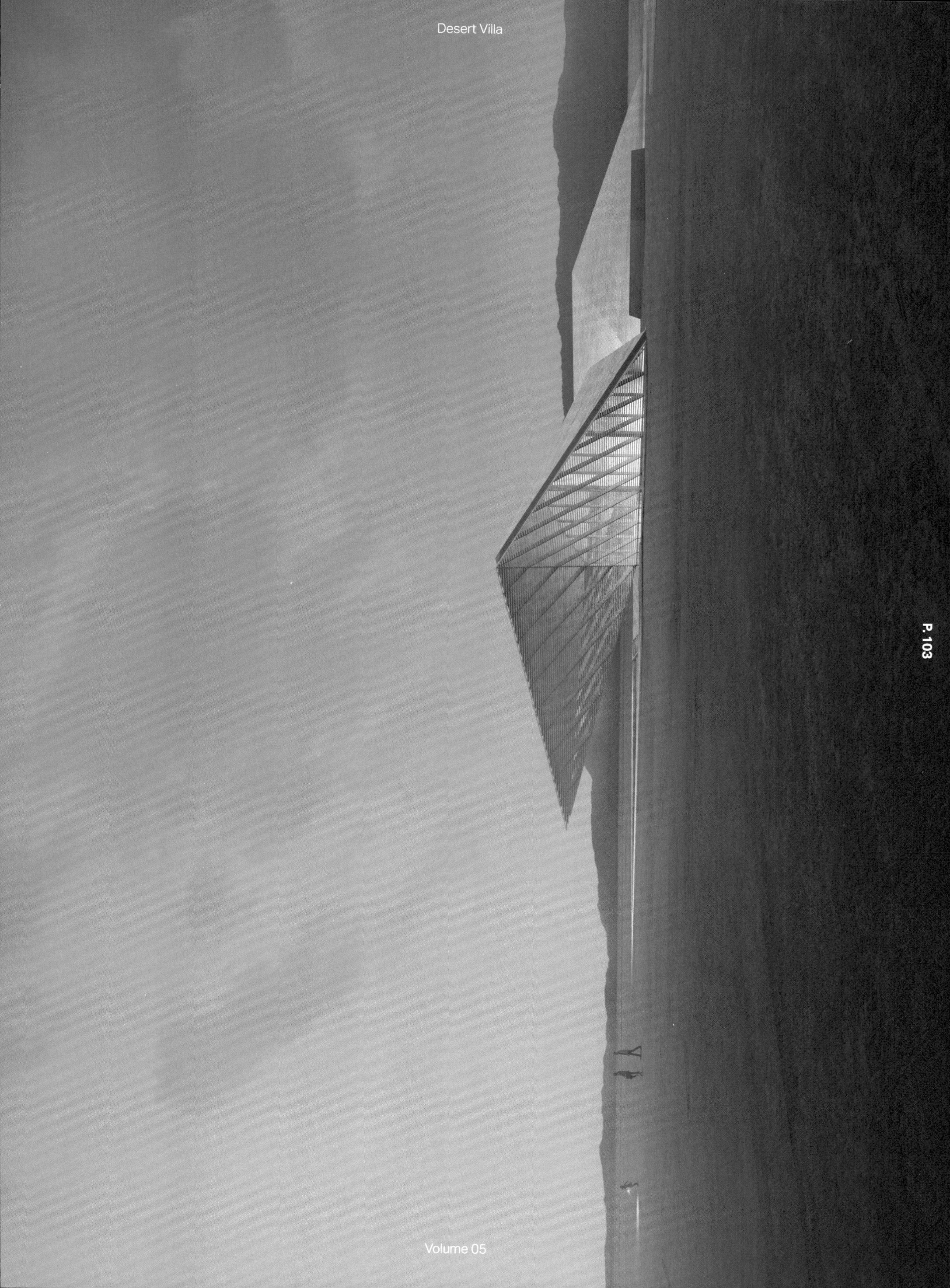

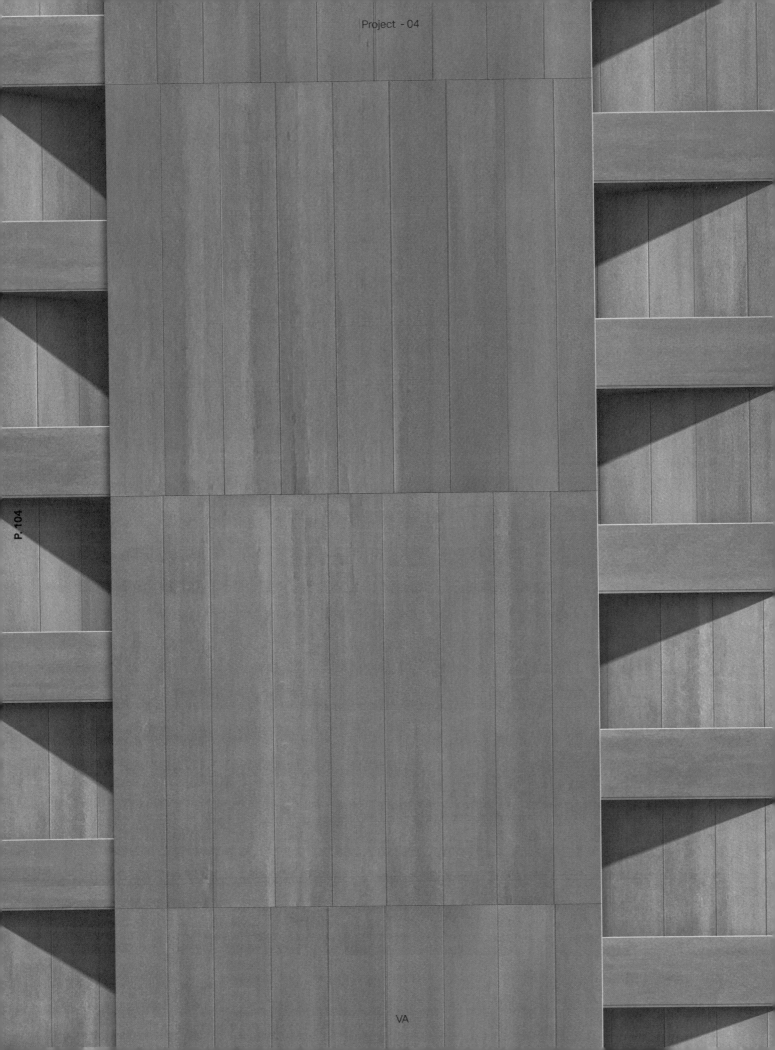

VA

MOUNTAIN LODGE

Trun, Switzerland

Standing within the large rectangular oculus, one has the option to view out over the vast rolling valley, or peer into the densely forested mountainside. Both vantage points offer a unique sublime experience.

This structure examines the characteristics of a tower located between a village of single-story cabins and some of the tallest mountains in the world. This juxtaposition of scale fosters an integration of short range and long range views and experiences, both within the tower and from a distance. The tower nestles into the mountainside, integrating it into the landscape as opposed to dominating it.

Standing within the large rectangular oculus, one has the option to view out over the vast rolling valley or peer into the densely forested mountainside. Both vantage points offer a unique sublime experience. The close-range view is an intimate closeup of the complexity and diversity of vegetation and wildlife. The other offers a view of scale and depth.

The hotel is located near the small Swiss village of Trun. This village is secluded and quaint, with a population of just over 1,000. The new hotel complements the local architecture with large glass facades and angular metal panels. Most notably, a large rectangular oculus overlooks the valley below. The structure makes no attempt to hide in the landscape, but instead rises 18 stories, emerging from the mountainside. A horizontally-oriented building would require significant environmental impact and manipulation. In contrast, the hotel goes vertical, minimizing its footprint while lightly touching the ground.

Much of the design of the Mountain Lodge enriches the user's journey. A winding single lane road leads from the small village up to the hotel. There is no parking lot or garage. Instead, visitors are dropped off under the amenities bridge. A series of walkways and stairs meander up the hill from the drop-off to the lobby, creating pockets of landscape and gardens throughout the hillside. These grounds are open to the public and mark the start of several trails leading off into the hillsides. Ultimately, these trails blur notions of public and private, and of natural and constructed landscapes.

The form is divided vertically into two functions, public and private spaces. The eastern half contains the guest rooms; the western half, the amenities. Each suite has a floor to itself and consists of three rooms: a bed, bath, and common area. Each room within the suite contains its own version of floor to ceiling glass with the bathroom cantilevering the tub off the east facade. In the upper suites, bridges are connected to individual suites within the oculus providing outdoor lounge space. The bridges double as an egress route to an emergency stairwell beyond.

Materials are minimal: just corten steel and glass. The warmth of the Corten steel contrasts the coolness of the glass, establishing a strong datum between the two materials. From a distance, this juxtaposition of solid and void is further enhanced. The corten steel contains layers of texture and tonal changes that only amplify with age relating to the weathered wood cottages in the village below. The warmth stands out from the heavily vegetated mountainside while not drawing too much attention to itself in such a pristine and undeveloped landscape.

Trun,
Switzerland

Elevation: 2,825 ft.

Population: 1,170

Annual High Temp: 77° F / 25° C

Annual Low Temp: 31° F / -1° C

Average Rain: 10 in. per year

Average Snow: 20.7 in. per year

**Proposed
Site**

Chapel

VA

0m

500

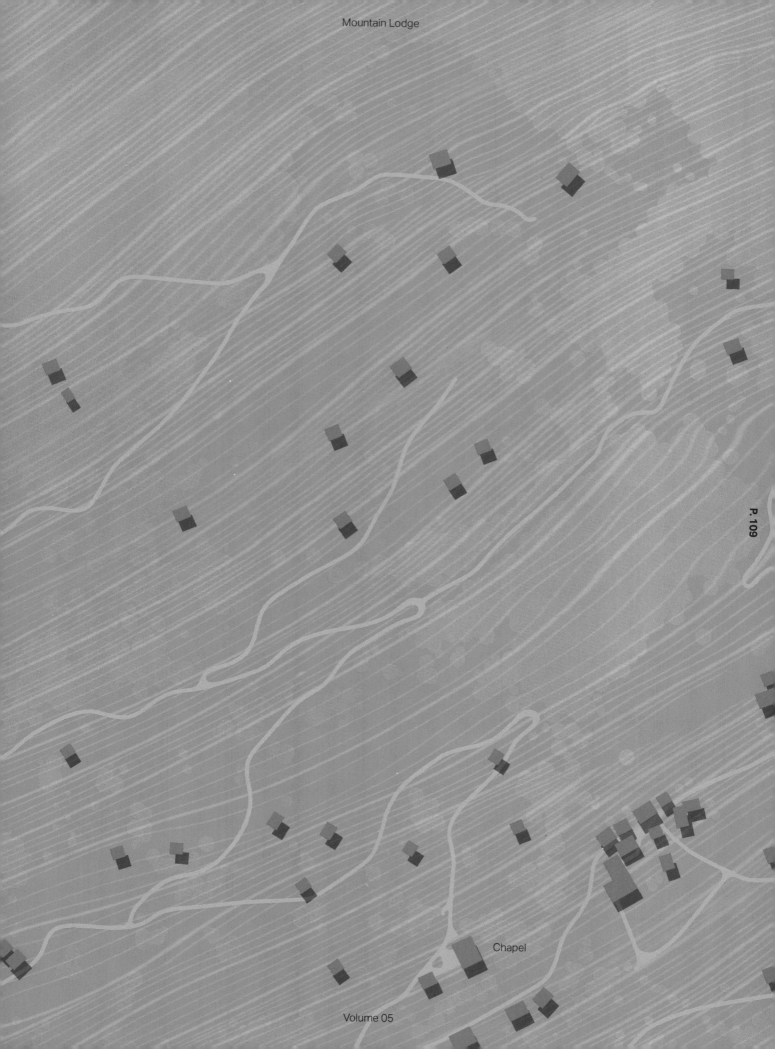

Chapel

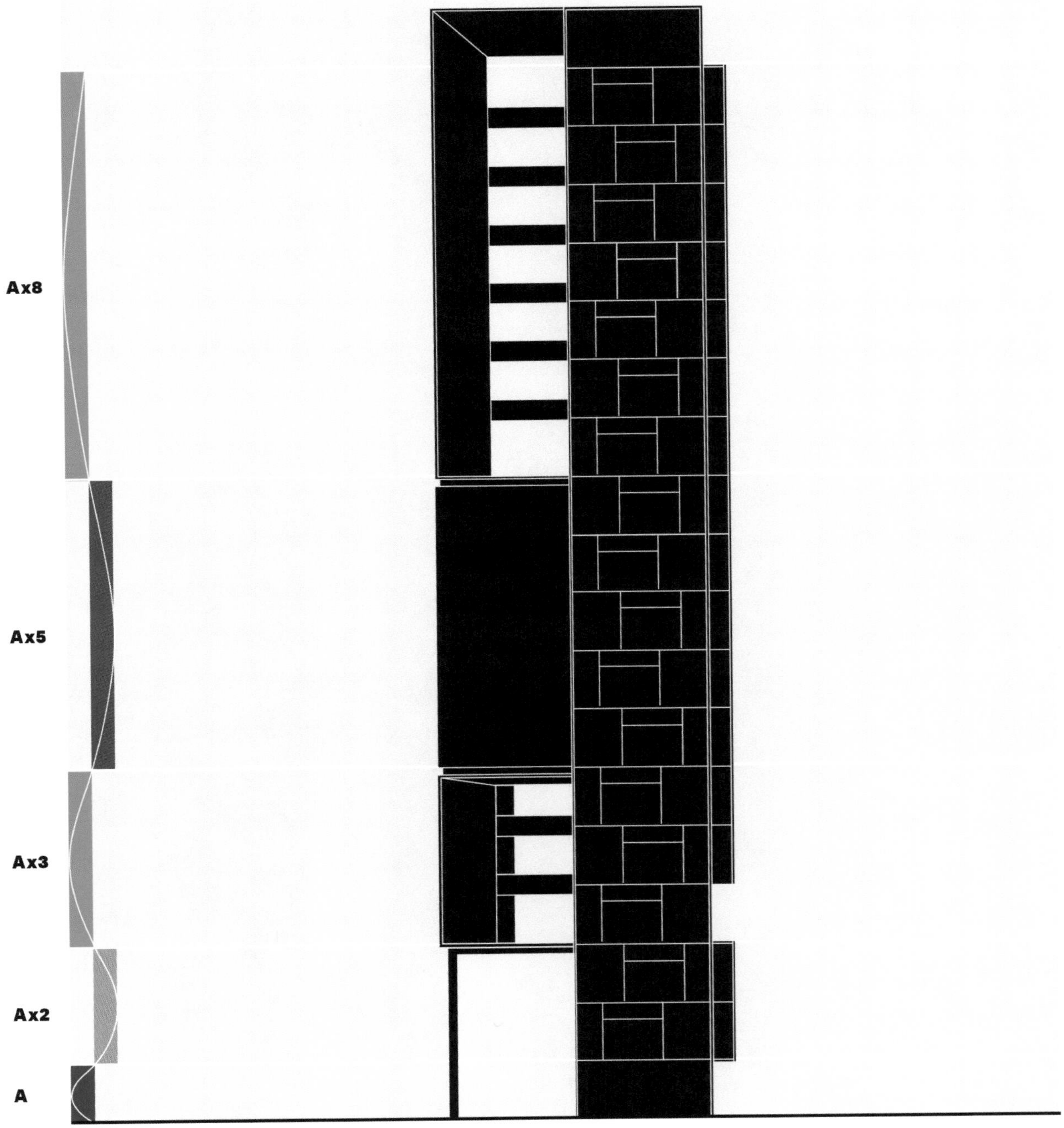

Ax8

Ax5

Ax3

Ax2

A

Fibonacci Proportions

A Fibonacci sequence was used as a way to organize the architectural forms vertically and provide a simple and subtle relationship to the solid and void elements in the form. While most notable in the overall facade, the sequence has been introduced into several other smaller scale details throughout the design.

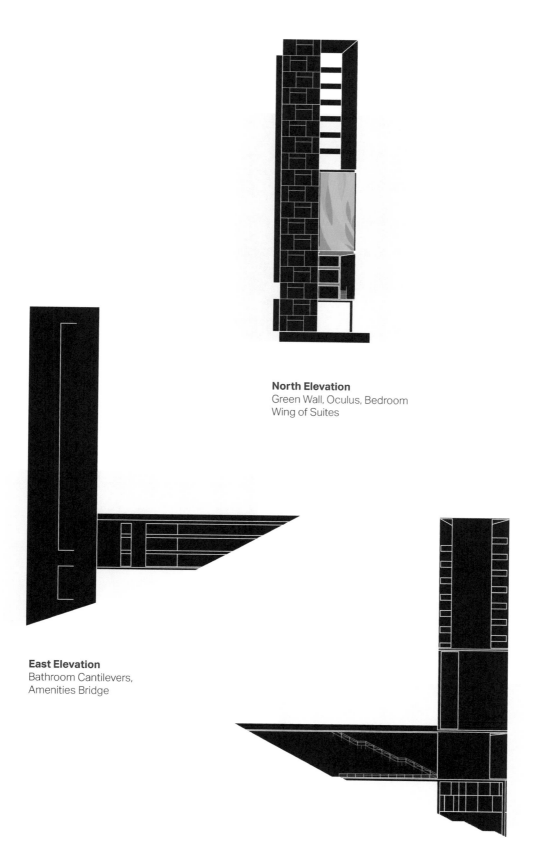

North Elevation
Green Wall, Oculus, Bedroom
Wing of Suites

East Elevation
Bathroom Cantilevers,
Amenities Bridge

West Elevation
External Stairs, Lobby,
Amenities Block

Lit from within, the oculus is a beacon. The corten steel facade glows warmly articulating a powerful geometric moment on the hillside.

Oculus Light: View from the South

Mechanical

Rooftop HVAC
Equipment

Oculus

Open Air Volume
Containing Suite
Balconies and Pool

Amenities Block

Gym, Conference
Rooms, and Service
Space

Entry Deck

Spill-Out Space for
Restaurants and
Multipurpose Rooms

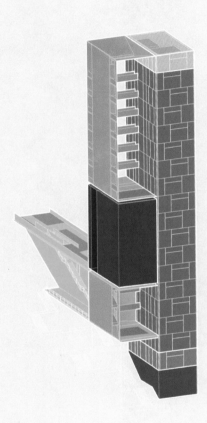

Guest Suites

Bedroom, Bath, and
Kitchen/Living Room

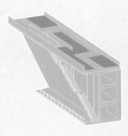

Bridge

Roof Garden,
Restaurants and
Multipurpose Space

Lobby

Check-in Desk and
Guest Lounge

Storage Base

Storage, Service, and
MEP Space

From afar, the form reveals itself and its function. Somewhat counterintuitively, the public space is signified by solid massing and materiality of the steel whereas the private space is wrapped through glazing. The transparent volumes appear to support the structure, while the heavy steel panels cantilever to the side, creating an asymmetrical balance.

Flowering Vegetation

Medium Height Shrub

Low Native Vegetation

Medium Native Vegetation

Pathway

Above:
Planting Site Plan

Right:
Rendered Site Plan

VA

Lower Gardens and Entrance: View from the West

Connector Bridge and Gardens

One of the most important elements of the lodge is the amenities bridge, providing an apex at the rooftop garden. Here, the transition from inside to outside is simple yet dramatic. Visitors may choose to meander the gardens or step directly into the mountainside forest. On the rear of the building, a multi-story green wall softens the transition from dense vegetation to the corten panels wrapping the building.

External Stair

An external stair was designed into the west facade of the tower. The form of the stair is distorted to maintain a chiseled edge at the oculus and designed to remain mostly hidden. As guests ascend and descend the upper portion of the tower, the landings occasionally reveal themselves to offer views to the west.

VA

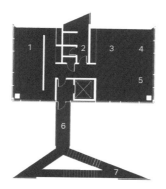

Guest Suite Plan

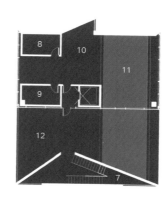

Pool Deck Plan

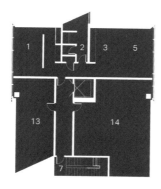

**Guest Suite and
Amenities Plan**

1. Bedroom
2. Bathroom
3. Kitchen
4. Dining
5. Living
6. Balcony
7. Stair
8. Men's Locker Room
9. Women's Locker Room
10. Lounge
11. Pool
12. Outdoor Lounge
13. Exercise Room
14. Multi-purpose Room
15. Lounge
16. Multi-purpose Room
17. Outdoor Lounge
18. Viewing Deck
19. Dining
20. Kitchen

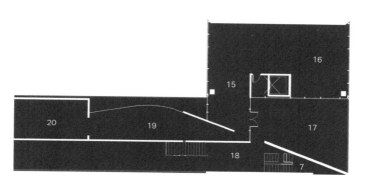

Bridge Plan

Above
View from the Southwest

Right
View from the Northeast

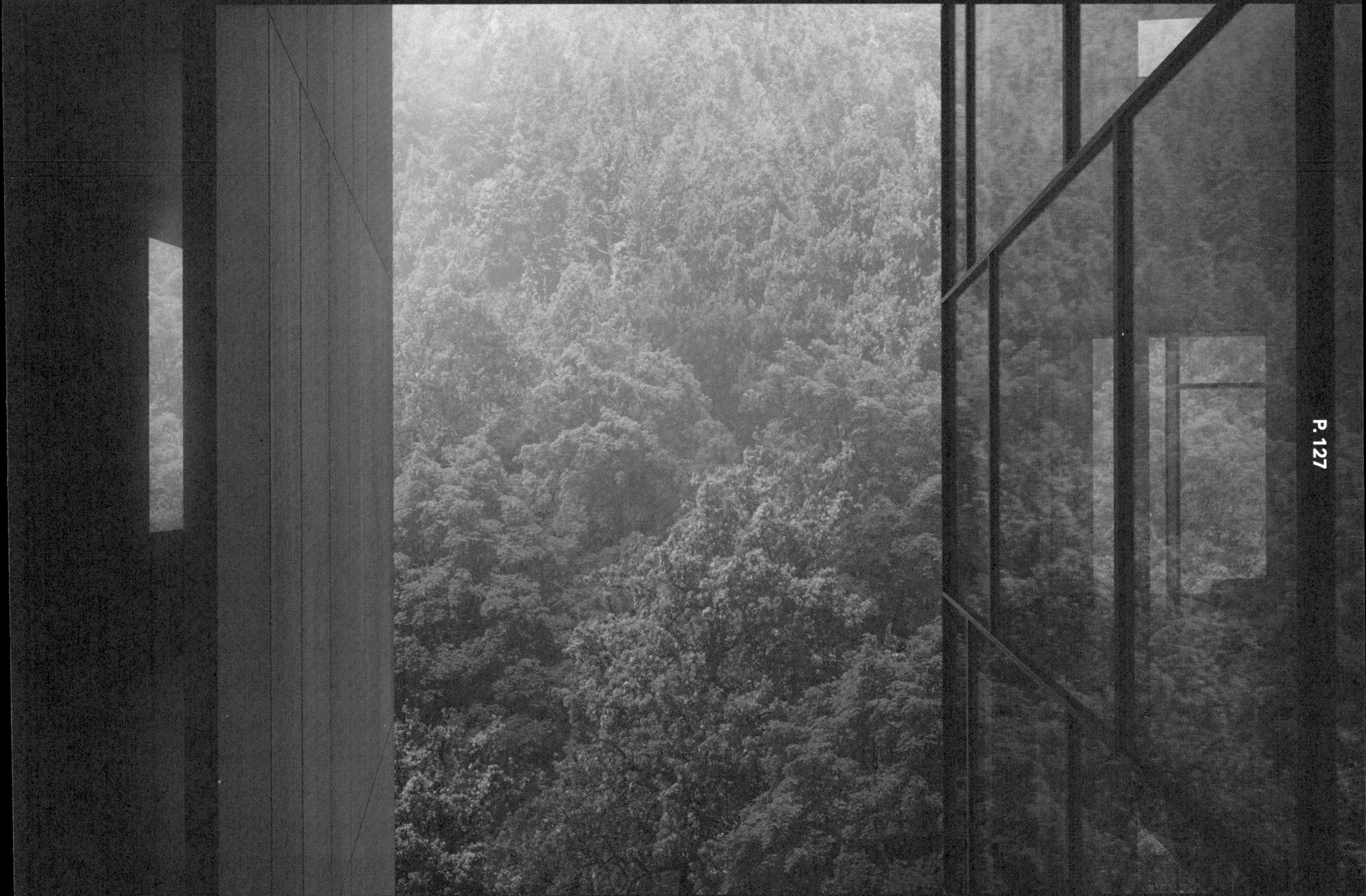

Best View Around: View from the West

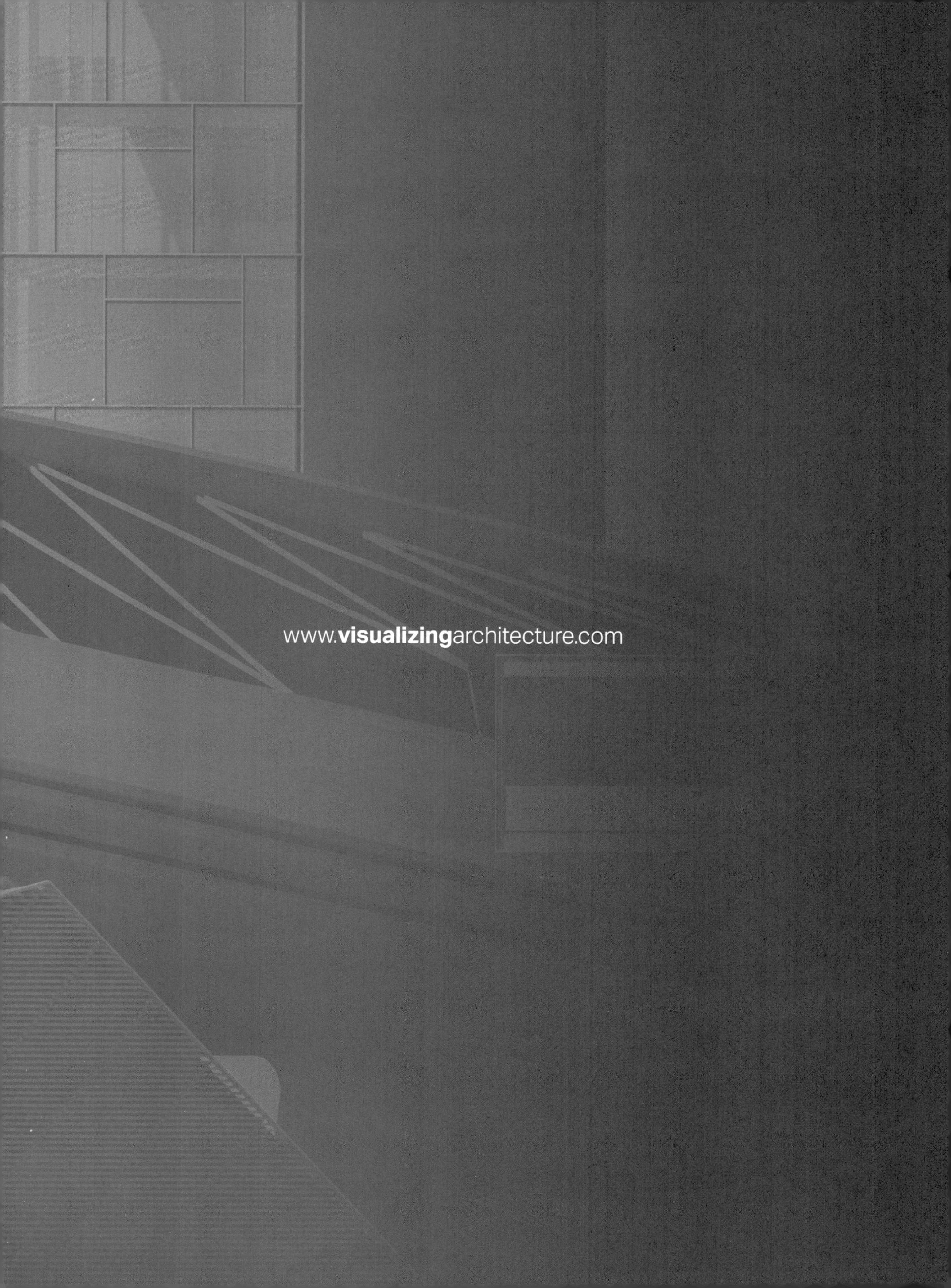
www.visualizingarchitecture.com

CPSIA information can be obtained at www.ICGtesting.com
Printed in the USA
BVIW121649121119
563596BV00004B/4

* 9 7 8 0 9 9 1 3 8 2 9 5 8 *